Before They Were President

BEFORE ABRAHAM LINCOLN WAS PRESIDENT

Gareth Stevens
PUBLISHING

By Theresa Morlock

Please visit our website, www.garethstevens.com. For a free color catalog of all our high-quality books, call toll free 1-800-542-2595 or fax 1-877-542-2596.

Library of Congress Cataloging-in-Publication Data

Names: Morlock, Theresa, author.
Title: Before Abraham Lincoln was president / Theresa Morlock.
Description: New York : Gareth Stevens, [2018] | Series: Before they were president | Includes index.
Identifiers: LCCN 2017017688| ISBN 9781538210567 (pbk. book) | ISBN 9781538210574 (6 pack) | ISBN 9781538210581 (library bound book)
Subjects: LCSH: Lincoln, Abraham, 1809-1865–Childhood and youth–Juvenile literature. | Presidents–United States–Biography–Juvenile literature.
Classification: LCC E457.32 .M67 2018 | DDC 973.7092 [B] –dc23
LC record available at https://lccn.loc.gov/2017017688

First Edition

Published in 2018 by
Gareth Stevens Publishing
111 East 14th Street, Suite 349
New York, NY 10003

Designer: Laura Bowen
Editor: Ryan Nagelhout

Photo credits: Cover, p. 1 (Abraham Lincoln) Fine Art/Corbis Historical/Getty Images; cover, p. 1 (cabin) Bob Thomas/Popperfoto/Getty Images; cover, pp. 1–21 (frame) Samran wonglakorn/Shutterstock.com; p. 5 S. Borisov/Shutterstock.com; pp. 7 (both), 15 (main), 21 (both) Everett Historical/Shutterstock.com; p. 9 J.L.G. Ferris/Library of Congress; p. 11 Kean Collection/Archive Photos/Getty Images; p. 13 Shrader, T./Library of Congress; p. 15 (inset) Kelly & Sons, New York/Library of Congress; p. 17 N. Currier/Library of Congress; p. 19 Bettmann/Getty Images.

Printed in China

CPSIA compliance information: Batch #CW18GS: For further information contact Gareth Stevens, New York, New York at 1-800-542-2595.

CONTENTS

Words in the glossary appear in **bold** type the first time they are used in the text.

HONEST ABE

Abraham Lincoln is one of the most highly respected Americans in history. As president, his strong leadership carried the United States through the Civil War. His **commitment** to freedom and fairness helped lead to the end of slavery.

Lincoln's **contributions** still affect the United States today. And his successes are even more impressive because he came from a **humble** background. Lincoln's journey to become America's 16th president in 1861 was long. He grew up very poor, but he was able to do great things by telling the truth and working hard.

Presidential Preview

One of Abraham Lincoln's nicknames was "Honest Abe." He had a **reputation** for being fair and truthful.

THE LINCOLN MEMORIAL WAS CREATED TO HONOR ABRAHAM LINCOLN'S CONTRIBUTIONS TO THE UNITED STATES. IT STANDS ACROSS FROM THE WASHINGTON MONUMENT ON THE NATIONAL MALL IN WASHINGTON, DC.

THE LINCOLN FAMILY

Abraham Lincoln was born in Kentucky on February 12, 1809. His family lived in a one-room log cabin with a dirt floor. His father, Thomas Lincoln, was a farmer who couldn't read or write. Abraham's mother was named Nancy, and his older sister was named Sarah.

When Abraham was 8, the family moved to Indiana. His mother died just a year later. Thomas soon remarried, and Abraham became very close to his new stepmother, Sarah. Sarah encouraged Abraham to read often.

Presidential Preview

As a boy, Lincoln was expected to help run the family's farm. He worked very hard clearing fields and caring for crops.

LINCOLN CABIN, KENTUCKY

THE LINCOLN FAMILY OWNED ONLY ONE BOOK—THE BIBLE.

ABE'S EDUCATION

Abraham's family couldn't afford to send him to school very often. Instead, he taught himself by reading. Abraham walked for miles to borrow books from his neighbors, including *Robinson Crusoe*, *Pilgrim's Progress*, and *Aesop's Fables*.

Young Abe was only allowed to read when his farmwork was done. His father also hired him out to neighbors to earn money for the family. Young Abe was known for being hardworking and good with an ax.

In 1830, the Lincoln family moved from Indiana to Illinois.

Presidential Preview

By the time he was 21, Abraham Lincoln stood 6 feet 4 inches (1.9 m) tall! He towered over most people and was very strong from years of hard work.

DURING HIS POLITICAL CAREER, ABRAHAM LINCOLN WAS SOMETIMES CALLED "THE RAIL-SPLITTER"——THAT'S SOMEONE WHO SPLITS WOOD TO MAKE FENCES. MANY PEOPLE LIKED THAT LINCOLN WAS RAISED ON A FARM AND WASN'T AFRAID OF HARD WORK.

9

A MAN OF MANY TALENTS

At age 22, Abraham left his family to make his own way. He worked on a flatboat, a small boat made of wood, carrying goods to sell. In 1831, he moved to New Salem, Illinois, where he took on several jobs. He became well-known to members of the community while working in the general store.

Lincoln continued to work as a rail-splitter, and he also worked as the town's postmaster and a county **surveyor**. During the Black Hawk War of 1832, Abraham served as a captain of the Illinois **militia**.

Presidential Preview

Lincoln was a champion wrestler! He was known for being tough and **wiry**.

ABRAHAM LINCOLN IS THE ONLY PRESIDENT TO HAVE A PATENT. HE INVENTED A TOOL TO IMPROVE BOAT TRAVEL.

A PRAIRIE LAWYER

After the Black Hawk War, Lincoln ran for a seat in the Illinois **legislature**. He lost the election, but he ran again in 1834 and won! He then decided to study law, passing the bar exam in 1836.

Abraham ran and won his seat in the state legislature three more times, serving terms in 1836, 1838, and 1840. In 1837, he moved to Springfield, the state capital of Illinois. In 1844, he opened his law practice with a partner, William Henry Herndon.

Presidential Preview

Lincoln's image as a country lawyer with a commitment to fairness appealed to voters. He was thought of as being a protector of the common man.

ABRAHAM LINCOLN CONTINUED TO PRACTICE LAW FOR 25 YEARS.

13

PERSONAL LIFE

In 1838, Abraham met Mary Todd, the woman who would become his wife. She was 10 years younger than he was and had grown up in a wealthy, important family. Mary and Abraham had very different personalities. They often argued and at one point even briefly canceled their plans to be married.

On November 4, 1842, Mary and Abraham married. They had four sons together—Robert, Edward, William, and Thomas, whom Abraham called Tad. Only two of the four Lincoln children would survive to adulthood.

Presidential Preview

Mary Todd was an **abolitionist**. During Abraham's presidency, many Southerners felt that she was a **traitor** because she didn't support the South's desire to keep slavery legal.

MARY TODD WAS WELL EDUCATED AND ACTIVE IN POLITICS.

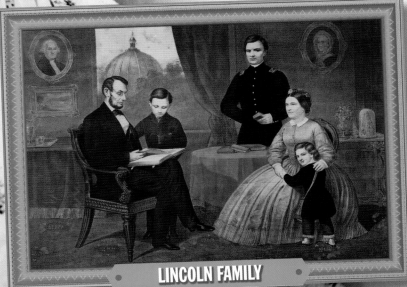

LINCOLN FAMILY

15

LINCOLN'S WHIG POLITICS

During his time in the Illinois legislature, Lincoln supported the Whig Party. The Whig Party supported the National Bank, didn't support increasing the power of the presidency, and was divided on the issue of slavery.

As a legislator, Lincoln argued against slavery but didn't support rights for free African Americans. In 1847, he was elected to the US House of Representatives as a Whig. In Congress, Lincoln spoke out against the Mexican-American War. In 1854, he ran for US Senate, but he lost the election.

Presidential Preview

In public, Lincoln often wore a tall stovepipe hat. He carried his most important papers in the hat's lining!

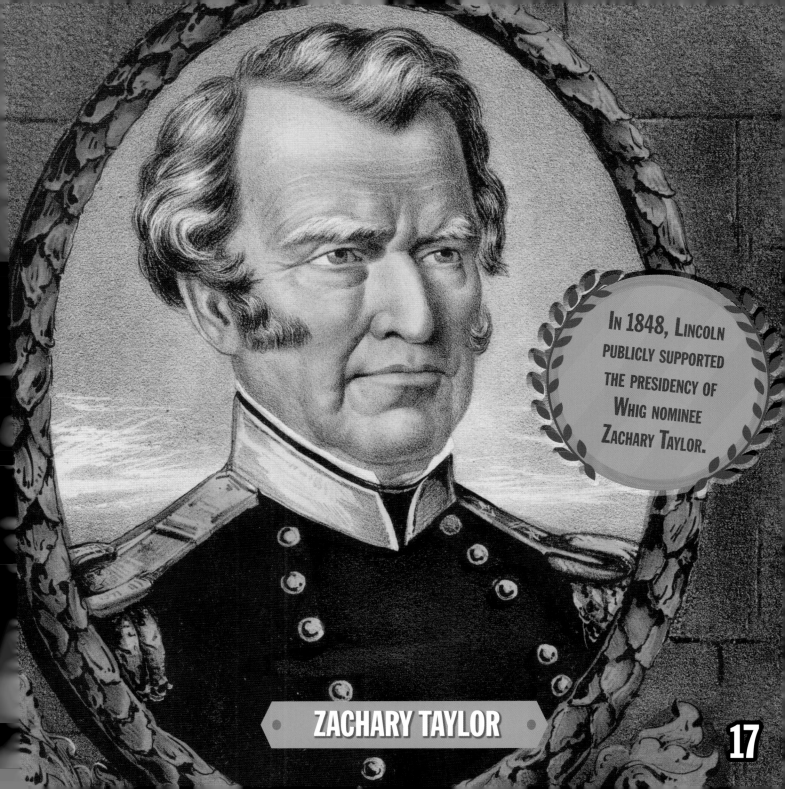

In 1848, Lincoln publicly supported the presidency of Whig nominee Zachary Taylor.

ZACHARY TAYLOR

17

THE LINCOLN-DOUGLAS DEBATES

After his failed campaign for Senate, Lincoln left the Whig Party to join the Republican Party, which didn't support slavery. In 1858, he again ran for a Senate seat against Democratic **candidate** Stephen Douglas.

Lincoln and Douglas took part in a series of **debates** about major issues of the time, particularly focused on slavery. The Lincoln-Douglas debates were very important to Lincoln's political career. Although Lincoln lost the election, he became known around the country as a great speaker and politician.

Presidential Preview

During the Lincoln-Douglas debates, Lincoln argued that slavery was against the founding beliefs of the Declaration of Independence.

THE LINCOLN-DOUGLAS DEBATES WERE A TURNING POINT IN BOTH LINCOLN'S LIFE AND AMERICAN HISTORY. THE MEN ARGUED OVER ISSUES THAT WOULD CHANGE THE FUTURE OF THE NATION.

PRESIDENT LINCOLN

In spring of 1861, the Republican Party began the hard process of choosing a candidate for the upcoming presidential election. At that time, the Democratic Party was very divided, and the Republicans saw this as a chance to gain support from states that were still undecided.

Well-known for his honesty and hard work, Abraham Lincoln made the perfect Republican candidate for the presidency. He won the election and became the 16th president of the United States on March 4, 1861.

Presidential Preview

Lincoln supported women's right to vote long before it became legal in the United States.

Lincoln's Life: A Timeline

1809	Abraham Lincoln is born in Kentucky.
1816	The Lincoln family moves to Indiana.
1818	Lincoln's mother, Nancy, dies.
1819	Lincoln's father, Thomas, marries Sarah Bush Johnston.
1830	The Lincoln family moves to Illinois.
1831	Abraham settles in New Salem, Illinois.
1832	Lincoln serves as captain of the militia in the Black Hawk War.
1834	Lincoln is elected to the Illinois General Assembly; he is reelected in 1836, 1838, and 1840.
1837	Lincoln is admitted to the Illinois Bar.
1837	Lincoln is elected to the US House of Representatives.
1842	Lincoln marries Mary Todd.
1844	Lincoln sets up a law practice with William Herndon.
1858	The Lincoln-Douglas debates occur.
1861	Lincoln is elected president of the United States.

LINCOLN CABIN, KENTUCKY

PRESIDENT LINCOLN

GLOSSARY

abolitionist: one who fights to end slavery

candidate: a person who runs for office in an election

commitment: the state of being faithful to a cause

contribution: the part played by a person to help bring something about

debate: a formal public discussion or argument

humble: of low rank or status

legislature: a lawmaking body

militia: a group of people who only fight when needed; a group of citizens who organize like soldiers in order to protect themselves

patent: a paper giving a person rights to an invention and stopping others from copying it

reputation: the ideas that people have about another person

surveyor: someone who examines and records the features of an area of land

traitor: a person who turns against their country

wiry: having a lean, strong form with an ability to bend

FOR MORE INFORMATION

Books

Gilpin, Caroline Crosson. *Abraham Lincoln*. Washington, DC: National Geographic Society, 2012.

Pascal, Janet B. *Who Was Abraham Lincoln?* St. Louis, MO: Turtleback Books, 2008.

Stevenson, Augusta. *Abraham Lincoln*. New York, NY: Aladdin, 2015.

Websites

Abraham Lincoln
whitehouse.gov/1600/presidents/abrahamlincoln
The White House website offers a short summary of the 16th president's upbringing and time in office.

Abraham Lincoln
history.com/topics/us-presidents/abraham-lincoln
This site examines Lincoln's life and achievements in the context of American history.

Abraham Lincoln the Man
nps.gov/linc/learn/historyculture/abraham-lincoln-the-man.htm
This National Park Service website has more information about Abraham Lincoln's life and presidency.

INDEX